This is Portland

Alexander Barrett & Andrew Dickson

Microcosm Publishing
Portland, OR

First printing of 6,000 copies, May 1, 2013
Second printing of 5,000 copies, January 15, 2014
Third printing of 7,000 copies, October 15, 2014
Fourth printing of 7,000 copies, March 15, 2016
Fifth printing of 7,000 copies, April 15, 2017

Second Edition, 7,000 copies, July 2018

Microcosm Publishing, 2752 N Williams Ave., Portland, OR 97227
MicrocosmPublishing.com
Carefully printed on post-consumer paper in the U.S.
Distributed by PGW and Turnaround UK
ISBN 978-1-62106-401-5

Library of Congress Cataloging-in-Publication Data

Names: Barrett, Alexander, 1983- author.
Title: This is Portland : the city you've heard you should like / Alexander
  Barrett.
Description: Portland, OR : Microcosm Publishing, 2017.
Identifiers: LCCN 2016050788 | ISBN 9781621064015 (pbk.)
Subjects: LCSH: Portland (Or.)--Description and travel. | Portland
  (Or.)--Social life and customs.
Classification: LCC F884.P84 B37 2017 | DDC 979.5/49--dc23
LC record available at https://lccn.loc.gov/2016050788

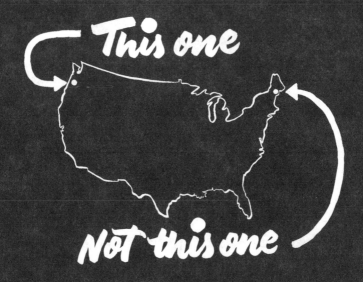

Before I moved to Portland, everyone told me it was the best city ever. When I asked them why, they couldn't be specific. I heard a lot of: "It just is."

This book is my attempt to be specific.

Not all of the things in this book are exclusive to Portland, but together, they'll give you an idea of how Portland makes me feel. This feeling will hopefully show you exactly why Portland, Oregon, is, hands down, the best city ever.

I wrote the introduction on the opposite page in 2011 after living in Portland for a year and a half. Since then, I've lived all over the United States and one very specific part of Asia. I've written another book called *This is Shanghai*, which you should consider picking up if you feel generally okay about this one.

I've been back to Portland several times, but each time I visit it feels a little different. When we decided to do a new version of *This is Portland*, I realized I couldn't rely on my memories of the city. I needed a ringer. I needed someone who's been on the ground in Portland. Someone who has fallen in love with this city and is in it for the long haul.

And I knew that somebody should be my friend and mentor Andrew Dickson.

I'll let him introduce himself.

Welcome to Portland.

Thanks Alex!

Okay everyone else,

When I graduated from college my friends who wanted to make it in the entertainment industry moved to Los Angeles, my friends who wanted to make it in journalism moved to New York, and my friends who wanted to overthrow the patriarchy moved to San Francisco (obviously this was awhile ago).

Me? I just wanted to have a good time.

So I moved to Portland. It was 1995. Gus Vant Sant was making cool films and it was gloriously affordable. I didn't like it at first. I made the mistake everyone does and moved here in fall when it starts to rain and everyone heads indoors. But before long I was playing in three bands, making my own movies and living with friends in a 5000 square foot warehouse for a few hundreds bucks a month.

Portland has changed substantially since then. You actually have to work a full-time job now to afford living here, and the price of a pint of beer has risen from $1.50 to three or four times that.

But the Portland spirit is still here. This is still the place to have a good time, whether you're here for a long weekend or the foreseeable future. So, if you're here and you're not enjoying yourself, take a drive out to the Gorge and go for a hike. Right now. And stop for a take-out burrito on your way out of town. You can be enjoying it sitting behind a towering waterfall while it's still warm.

the Rain

When you start talking about visiting or moving to Portland, people are going to warn you about the rain. Apparently, the consensus among everyone I know is that they'd like to live in Portland, but they just can't deal with the oppressive, ever-present rain.

Here is Portland's greatest secret: It doesn't rain that much. It's a little gloomy for most of the winter, but it only occasionally gets really serious about raining. It drizzles, sure, but anyone can handle a drizzle.

I don't want to seem paranoid, but there is absolutely a conspiracy at work here. Portlanders over-hype the rain in order to keep outsiders from moving in. When tourists visit in summer and think Portland is a paradise on earth and the answer to all of their problems, the locals say, "Sure, but this only lasts for four months. The rest of our life here is a wet, cloudy, living hell. Save yourself! Get out while you still can!" And then the tourists back away slowly and leave the city forever, allowing the locals to stretch their legs, and making the lines at Pine State Biscuits much shorter.

It might not be ethical, but it works.

Okay, I started writing this in January. It is now March. It rains plenty here. It rains about 37.5 inches a year. I'm not part of this conspiracy. I am actually annoyed. It is oppressive. It is ever-present. I'm told it won't stop until the Fourth of July. Save yourself! Get out while you still can!

Reading this over, I'm worrying that I may be focusing too much on the weather right off the bat. Weather shouldn't make a city. But in Portland's case, it really does. Everything about Portland changes with the seasons. And by seasons, I'm talking about Rain and Summer. During the rain, Portland is dreary, but it's still a great city. During the summer, it borders on heaven.

More on that later.

One more observation about the rain: Portland is full of cool people. Raincoats are not cool. How do cool people stay cool in the rain? They get really wet, that's how.

the Sun

When the sun comes out in Portland, the city changes.

All spring, there are hints of how good it's going to be. It's a Saturday morning, you walk outdoors and there are no clouds. Suddenly, you see people emerging from their homes, looking at the sky, confused. Everyone just stands there, soaking up the vitamin D. A few minutes later, they snap out of their stupor. They say: "Oh. Outside! I get it! This is how life used to be!" Sunglasses are uncovered, bikes are taken out of storage, and men remember what women are. People point their cameras toward the sky, take a picture of pure blue and immediately post it online. The caption will be a series of capitalized vowels followed by a field of exclamation points. But this is just a tease, because it will rain again.

The city has to wait for the Fourth of July. After that, there won't be rain for four months. That four months is what Portland is all about.

This city wears its Winter like a badge of honor. There are six hundred thousand people who have all agreed to live through a damp, eight-month nightmare. Because they know that when it finally comes to an end, they will experience perfection: the Portland Summer.

The Portland Summer is many things, but mostly, it's:

Barbecues,

Barbecues,

Barbecues,

Barbecues,

and

Barbecues.

Barbecues every night of the week and three times a day on weekends. It is the ultimate summer, because you've earned it.

You stuck out that winter and you were wet for eight months. This is yours by right and you will stand tall with a hamburger in one hand and a cheap beer in the other.

the year's
FIRST
Ray of
SUNSHINE

City of Roses

There are two possible reasons for Portland's official nickname.

1. In 1871, Leo Samuel moved to Portland. He always kept perfectly groomed rose bushes on his front lawn. A pair of clippers sat next to the bushes so passersby could snip off a flower and take it with them, perhaps for use as a boutonniere. In 1906, Samuel founded the Oregon Life Insurance Company.

2. During an 1888 Episcopal Church convention, someone said something about Portland being "the City of Roses." The name didn't really go anywhere for the next seventeen years. Then, Mayor Harry Lane spoke before the 1905 Lewis and Clark Centennial Exposition and declared that the city needed a festival of roses. Two years later, the festival of roses began. It and the nickname have been going strong ever since.

Benson Bubblers

For definitive proof that Portland is an easy place to have a good time, take a trip downtown and behold the Benson Bubbler.

It's a water fountain.

But hold on, there's more.

A businessman named Simon Benson noticed a few too many people getting too drunk at lunch. So he gave the city some money and gave life to the world's most wonderful water fountain.

Instead of making you press a rusted knuckle of a metal button so hard that it mangles your thumb, the Benson Bubblers' water flow 24/7, doing a delectable dance of hydration. Just try not to take a sip.

And you know how some water fountains are super low to the ground and only give you a miserly half-inch flow so you inevitably stoop over hurting your back and then bang your teeth on cold metal? Not the Benson Bubbler. It stands tall and bubbles a full two proud high inches allowing you to wet your whistle in style.

And because who wants to wait in line for a drink of water, each of the fifty-two bubblers that dot downtown have four different spouts so that you and your friends can all quench your thirst at the same time.

So go ahead, forget your water bottle at home, get a little parched.

Benson's got you covered.

the "White Stag" Sign

The Sun has set on the East side. You're wearing presentable clothing, ready for a night out in Portland. You hop in a car and head out. Then, halfway across the Burnside Bridge, you see it: a white stag atop a neon outline of the state of Oregon. Quickly, words appear: Portland. Oregon. And they sparkle. In that moment, you know that you are about to have an incredible evening.

But that sign wasn't always a celebration of all things Portland. First erected as an advertisement for sugar and later updated to a celebration of sportswear, the sign has undergone many changes due to landmarking, building ownership, electric bills, and all kinds of other things that aren't fun to explain.

Just know that if you go to Portland, it will be on and waiting for you.

And yes, they still put a red nose on the Stag during the holiday season.

1940

1950

1957

1997

2010

Strip Clubs

Portland is home to more strip clubs per capita than any other U.S. city. This is true. Portland has more strip clubs per capita than Las Vegas.

At first, it doesn't make sense. "All I can see here are coffee shops and record stores." Then after a week, they start revealing themselves to you. And they don't stop. There are well over 50 strip clubs in the greater metropolitan area. It is at once awe-inspiring and just a touch shady. It really is mostly awe-inspiring, though.

So, why? Why does the most pleasant, quiet city in the United States have more professional naked ladies than anywhere else? There are two reasons. First, the Oregon state constitution protects first amendment rights like crazy. In 1987, the Oregon Supreme Court found that full nudity and lap dances are protected speech in Henry v. Oregon Constitution.

Second, Portland used to be a sketchy place. Back around the time of the gold rush, Portland was basically lawless. It was exactly the kind of place that could support a vibrant sex industry. Over the years, as the city got safer, the strip clubs remained.

They're just a part of the culture now. In many areas, it's easier to get to a strip club than it is to get to the supermarket. And that doesn't bother anybody. I'm sure it bothered somebody at some point. The Henry from "Henry v. Oregon Constitution," I bet he was bothered. But people like Henry have been shouted down for years. By now, they've either learned to accept it or moved away.

There's something funny about knowing that no matter where you are, you could be at a strip club in ten minutes. Many times, I've asked my coworkers: "What are you up to tonight?" And they say: "I don't know. Nothing. I'm pretty tired and I think I'm getting sick." A half an hour later, I'm getting drunk texts from the rack at Sassy's.

The next day, when I ask how they ended up there, they just shrug.

It's just what you do.

Weirdness

The city used to be awash in bumper stickers that read, "Keep Portland Weird."

But then people started to realize that Austin came up with that catchphrase first and they were pissed that Portland was getting so much mileage out of it. So we've slowly but surely replaced most of them with "Keep Portland Beered" bumper stickers.

Which feels accurate. A lot of Portland's weirdness has aged up or sadly been priced out and moved on. But there is more beer than ever. There is still some weird to be found here, but for better or worse, it's just really not that weird anymore.

The only people who haven't gotten the memo are the realtors and insurance agents who aggressively compete with each other via billboards and bus ads to prove how weird they are in the hopes of getting people to hire them.

Here's the thing:

I like weird people. I don't mind being served by a weird bartender, or going to see a weird artist perform. But if I'm going to buy a house, which will probably be the biggest and most stressful purchase of my life, I don't want to deal with a weirdo. I just want to deal with a non-creative, body art-free human being.

I want boring.

But after writing this chapter and sending it to Joe, the publisher, he mentioned that the realtor who sold him a house in Portland put a lot of emphasis on the presence of ghosts. And yet he says that he was otherwise happy with his realtor's expertise.

So I guess I'm the weird one here.

AT LEAST THERE'S STILL A NAKED BIKE RIDE!

Bands

If you live in Portland and you aren't in a band, people will look at you funny at concerts. They'll ask: "So, when are you going up?" And you'll say: "Oh, no, I just came to hear some music."

Then they'll give you the stink eye and back away slowly.

Portland is a city divided. In all kinds of ways metaphorically, but in only one way physically.

Flowing right through the middle of town is a little thing called the Willamette River. As far as rivers go, it's a pretty good one. Not too fast, not too slow. Just the right temperature for a dip on the hottest day of summer. And unlike some other rivers that will remain nameless, not quite wide enough to disassociate the land beyond each of its banks. Sure, Portland's East and West sides have slightly differents energies, but they still feel like the same place.

I guess it's partly to do with the river's width, but a lot of the credit should go to the twelve bridges in the metropolitan area.

Twelve. That's a lot of bridges. A lot of bridges with a lot of different styles and a lot of different feelings. Let's take a closer look at the structures that give Portland its most obvious and arguably most appropriate nickname.

The St. Johns Bridge is bright green and designed in a happy, simplified gothic style. When you begin to cross, it feels as if you are entering a joyous cartoon kingdom.

The Burlington Railroad Bridge is for trains only, so it's stunningly-close-to-downtown and low-to-the-river views are exclusively the purview of Amtrak riders and freight train hoppers.

The Fremont Bridge looks like the trajectory of a skipping stone.

Broadway

The Broadway Bridge's erector set-esque construction makes you feel like you're in the middle of a car chase through gritty city streets in the 70s. Except for the fact that it's bright red and has a luxurious bike lane.

Steel

The Steel Bridge features a pedestrian walkway that runs across its bottom, getting you as close as possible to the Willamette while remaining dry.

As the bridge with the best view of Portland's White Stag sign, the Burnside Bridge might be the most iconic Portland bridge experience. Plus, when a boat has to pass, the bridge opens and you see the street rise ninety degrees in front of your face. Others do that too, but somehow not quite as fantastically.

The Morrison Bridge has options. This isn't a simple couple of lanes that goes from one side of the river to the other. Want to get on the 5? How about Belmont? Or maybe Southeast Water Avenue? Maybe Southwest Washington is your speed. And if it's not, there's always Pacific Highway West. No matter what, this bridge has you covered.

The Hawthorne Bridge has two kinds of lanes. The inside lanes are paved and give you a perfectly smooth ride. Rumor has it that the metal grates of the outside lanes were installed upside down, creating some not-so-beautiful music as you drive across.

My advice: stay left.

The double-decker Marquam Bridge is part of I-5, making it the bridge least likely to be name-dropped in an acoustic folk song tribute to Portland because the I-5 is more of a California Interstate.

Tilikum Crossing is the newest bridge and the only one closed to cars. Perfect for biking, walking, skateboarding, and unicycling.

The Ross Island Bridge is more about where it goes than what it is. Head East and you'll hit Mt. Hood. Head West and you'll hit the coast.

Thanks to the completion of a brand new Sellwood Bridge right next to the falling apart old one, you no longer have to participate in any kind of superstitious ritual to ensure you make it across alive.

Auctions?

Yes, auctions.

Portland is one of the auction epicenters of the country. Specifically auctions to raise money for good causes. Nearly every single non-profit organization and school in town has an annual fundraiser with an auction.

If you're picturing a stuffy wood-walled room filled with bored rich people and an auctioneer as pretentious as they are unexcitable, pick up the remote and turn off the James Bond movie.

These are raucous affairs with lots of booze, raffle prizes, live music and inevitably, at least at the school auctions, two parents who have had too much of that booze suddenly realizing they cannot go home without their first grader's fingerpaint masterpiece getting into a spirited bidding war that can soar into four figures.

While the live auction is the main event, the real deals are on the silent auction tables. That's where local businesses support their community by donating gift certificates and services. It's a chance to get Trailblazers tickets and a signed ball, a Mt. Hood cabin for the weekend, or dinner at ¿Por Qué No? often for under market value. And you get to feel good about yourself in the process.

SE v. NE

At this point in the book, you're probably ready to move to Portland. Congratulations, I think this is a great decision. Now you're probably wondering where in the city I think you should move. That's easy. I'm an east side guy.

Portland is split right down the middle by the Willamette River. On the West Side, you'll find the downtown area. It's the part of the city that looks like a city. The Northwest is more residential. Things close early there. The Southwest has Portland State University. There's a hospital down there, too. I'll be honest with you, I went down there once for a party and I've never been back. That party got real weird.

On the east side, it doesn't even feel like you're living in a city. It feels like a sleepy, small town that decided to get cool. Most of it is residential, with pockets of shops, restaurants, parks, bars, movie theaters, and coffee. A lot of coffee.

If you work on the west side, it's more of a hike, but I like riding my bike over the river every morning. And if you're meeting friends for a night on the town, you just ride over Burnside Bridge and see a tiny, little metropolis unfolding before you. From half a mile away, you can see the whole city, all lit up.

It's like the beginning of *Bladerunner*. Except way more adorable.

Now you're probably saying: "Sounds great. East side. You've sold me. So should I live in Northeast or Southeast?" That's where things start to get tricky.

Both have amazing shops, restaurants, parks, bars, movie theaters, and coffee. A lot of coffee. They are equally fantastic places to be. I've lived in both and I can't choose. Please don't make me choose. Most people who live on the east side, however, have a very strong opinion on the matter. And I think I know the reason why.

If you ask someone who lives in the Northeast, they'll say the Northeast is better. If you ask someone who lives in the Southeast, they'll say the Southeast is better. And it's simply because they want to drink close to their house.

If you live in the Northeast and a friend is having a get together in the Southeast, you either have to bike or drive. Let's face it, if you're going to the get together, you're gonna drink. And when you get to that four beer mark, nobody wants to deal with a bus.

If you're asking a friend where to move, their goal is to get you to move close to them so there's less a chance of you having a party elsewhere.

My advice: Throw a dart at a map. You'll be happy either way.

I'd like to preface this by saying that even after a year and a month in Portland, I still do not have a tattoo. I'll try my best not to sound like an unhip suburban mom.

In Portland, there are twelve tattoo parlors for every hundred-thousand people. That's a lot of tattoo parlors. How can that many businesses sustain themselves in one, medium-sized city? You'll know why as soon as you walk down any street.

Tattoos are everywhere. And they're on every single kind of person.

There's a janitor at the school down the street with the cover of the *Dungeon Master's Guide* on his forearm.

Your company's IT guy has an ice cream sundae on his chest.

One night, you'll be out to a fancy meal and your server will have the *Thrasher Magazine* logo tattooed across his or her neck.

I once bought a book at a yard sale from a mom with a tattoo of a hippie mushroom on her face. Surprisingly, her children seemed well balanced. (Okay, I got a little bit suburban mom just then. Sorry.)

Tattoos are another holdover from Portland's wild west history. Sure, the city has gotten a whole lot more pleasant, but its people want to remind you that Portland is and always will be a city of badasses.

The Most Portland Thing I Have Ever Seen

I have witnessed two events that tie for the title of "the most Portland thing I have ever seen." Feel free to judge for yourself.

1. As I rode my bike west on Southeast Ankeny Street, I approached what I thought was another bike and prepared to pass. When I got closer, I saw that the rider was sitting three feet above me, but this wasn't a "tall bike." As I passed, I finally knew what I was looking at: a giant unicycle. This unicycle's rider was wearing khakis, a polo shirt, and had a padded messenger bag on his back. It wasn't just a giant unicycle. It wasn't even the Unipiper*. It was a giant commuter unicycle.

There was even a fender connected to the back seat. This guy planned to ride through the rain all winter.

So why is this a perfect symbol for Portland? It's alternative, business casual, stubbornly ecofriendly, it doesn't care how stupid it looks, and it involves the suffix "cycle." He should be the Grand Marshal of the Rose Parade. The city's flag should just be his picture. This guy should get a key to the city and his likeness should be engraved on the key's side.

2. It was spring. Somehow, the sun was out, which meant that everyone was on the street. I was walking west over the Burnside Bridge to meet some friends. Up ahead, a tricycle for hire with a two-passenger back seat, aka a "Pedicab," was approaching slowly.

The Pedicab driver was just starting to climb the bridge's incline, and was having a pretty difficult time. I looked in the backseat. In it were two morbidly obese Goth women. They were both smoking. The driver would pedal once, recover for a second, and then pedal again. I really felt for him, but what could I do?

Just then, an elderly couple began to walk across the bridge. They looked like they were enjoying a lovely day. It was easy to see that they were runners. They had the shoes, they had the hats, and they were both in great shape. As soon as the elderly man saw the Pedicab driver struggling, he ran out into the street, greeted the two Goth women, and started pushing the Pedicab up the hill. I had to stop myself from cheering.

So why is this a perfect symbol for Portland? It involves two alternative ladies, running culture, ecofriendliness, a man going beyond the call of politeness, and the suffix "cycle." I felt like taking the whole group to Voodoo Donuts, then over to Stumptown, where we'd sit and laugh and feel good about our city.

*the UNIPIPER rides his UNICYCLE through the streets of Portland wearing a KILT, a CAPE, and a DARTH VADER MASK while playing BAGPIPES that are also FLAMETHROWERS. He should run for MAYOR.

Fancy Junk Food

"Sometimes foods." My mom had been warning me about them since I was old enough to pull a chair over to the refrigerator, open the freezer, and get my hands on those sweet popsicles. They're the foods you only have once in a while, because if you had them all the time, you'd be fat.

Portland has turned "sometimes foods" into high art.

It's turned "sometimes" into "all the time."

Wherever you go, you'll find foods that you definitely shouldn't be eating, but hey, you're finally standing in front of this place that you've heard so much about and they have that maple bacon whatever that everyone's been telling you to try. So you do.

And you justify it because hey, it's artisanal.

I really like running. I'd go as far as saying that I am a runner. In Portland, it rains a lot. I'm not crazy about running in the rain. I'm kind of a baby. I do not, however, mind eating fancy junk food in the rain. That suits me just fine.

This is a problem.

One day, I was at Lovely's Fifty Fifty, eating a transcendental salted caramel ice cream cone. One of my friends said they preferred the salted caramel at Salt & Straw. What were we going to do, not go to Salt and Straw and get another ice cream?

Needless to say, I have gained weight in Portland and it has been delicious.

Consider yourself warned.

Cheap Movies (and Beer)

In Portland, it's easier to pay $3 for a movie than it is to pay $10. This is especially true in the Southeast. There are two second-run theaters within three blocks of my apartment. Within a mile, there are another two. If I want to see a new movie, I have to get in the car and drive at least three miles to a mall or somewhere very close to a mall. It's not nice there. And the worst part is, once I get there, I won't be able to find the two things that make Portland's second-run theaters truly great: pizza and beer.

For less than the price of a first-run movie ticket, popcorn, and a soda, you can get a second-run movie ticket, a full meal of totally satisfactory pizza, and you can be drunk. What a beautiful idea! When you walk out of a late movie at the Laurelhurst Theater on SE 28th and Burnside, you're greeted with a jar sitting next to all the pizza the theater couldn't sell that night. There's a sign on the jar inviting you to pay whatever you want for a slice. The first time I saw this, I almost cried.

Whenever a magazine comes out with a "most livable cities in America" list, Portland is always on it. The articles talk about biking, dining, public transportation.

I read an article recently that said Portland's livability index is 100.3. I don't know what that means, but I guarantee you 100 whatevers of those 100.3 whatevers is eating a pizza and having a beer at the movies.

Full disclosure: I lied a little bit. Not all of these theaters have pizza and beer. There's one that doesn't: The Avalon. Instead, it has a full arcade where every game costs a nickel. The movies only cost $3.50, too.

What a nightmare.

PDX

Every day is sunny at 39,000 feet.

PDX is the airport code for Portland International Airport.

It's an adorable airport. Maybe I've only ever arrived at off-hours, but it's never taken more than 10 minutes to get through security and into one of its lovely breweries.

It's been named the best airport in the U.S. by *Travel + Leisure* at least four times. Between its gates, you'll find smaller versions of Portland staples like Stumptown Coffee, the Hollywood Theatre, the Country Cat, and Powell's Books. You may have even purchased this book there. If so, welcome! Or goodbye, thanks for coming!

For a while, PDX featured a carpet that captured the imagination of everyone who walked over it. Look it up. It was a sign that you had arrived in a place where things were different.

The new carpet is, too; just give yourself some time to warm up it.

Portland is book crazy.

We have a book festival that ten thousand people attend, we treat our many famous authors like rock stars, and we're arguably the epicenter of zine culture and independent publishing. We even elected a bookstore owner to our city council.

Oh, and we have the biggest bookstore in the world. Go ahead, try walking through the downtown's Powell's City of Books without a map. We'll send a search party in if we haven't seen you in a week.

In other cities, parents post pictures of the kids playing sports. Here, our social media feeds are full of pictures of kids competing in the Oregon Battle of the Books, where teams compete to answer questions about a slate of sixteen different books they've each read.

Why is there so much reading, writing, and book loving? For the answer, look no further than your window. Is it raining? If so, great, go grab that book you've been looking forward to and find a quilt to put over your feet. It makes sense, now, doesn't it?

Bikes

Portland has a lot of bikes.

Beer

Portland has a lot of beer.

Beards

Portland has a lot of beards.

Tater Tots

In Portland, every bar that serves liquor is required by law to serve at least three hot food items and two cold food items. This is probably why the gastropub has become such an institution. These are bars with great beer, great food, and great atmosphere.

But what if you don't care about great food? What if you just want to sell watery beer and booze? What if you just want to open a shithole?

Tots.

Tater tots are cheap and easy. All you need to do is open a bag and dump them into a Fry-o-lator. You can even leave them in too long if you want. Past golden brown and on their way to black is a Portland standard. It doesn't matter, I really won't mind because I'm definitely drunk and anything you put in front of me is going to be manna from heaven.

"Are these spicy tots or regular, because I ordered regular," I might ask as you place a basket in front of me.

"Oh, these are spicy let me just get you a…" you won't finish your sentence. I don't care. The basket will be snatched from your hands and my mouth will be full of delicious fried potato cylinders within seconds. Your tip will be generous.

I know that tater tots are ubiquitous. They are American. Portland doesn't own them. But for me, no night out in Portland is complete without a basket. No matter where I go, they'll always remind me of great times, great people, and riding the bus home, completely satisfied and sometimes asleep.

Oh, and for all you new bar owners: while you've got that Fry-o-lator going, why not throw in a bag of fries and a few corn dogs? There's your three hot menu items.

Oh, right, you need two cold items. How about a bag of chips and a plate of iceberg lettuce coated with the cheapest ranch dressing you can possibly find?

Perfect.

Chickens

If you have a backyard and you don't keep chickens, many will suspect you of being a Republican.

the Fish Hatchery

Listen, I know the hatchery isn't in Portland, but it's less than an hour drive and I want to talk about it. So, all the purists who were reading this expecting to only hear about things in the Portland metropolitan area, you just deal with it for two pages.

One day, I had nothing to do. I was getting antsy and just needed to get into my car and drive somewhere. I looked at a map and said: "Bonneville Dam. I've heard of that. That sounds like a guided tour I can get behind."

So I drove. Just before I got to the Dam, I saw a sign pointing towards a fish hatchery. I took no notice and continued. An hour later, I had finished a guided tour and discovered something about myself: I have a wide spectrum of interests, but unfortunately, guided tours of dams don't fall anywhere near it. I went back to Portland.

The next day, I went to work and told the tale of my non-adventure. Every person I talked to asked if I had gone to the fish hatchery. I told them no. Then they all exploded.

"WHAT ABOUT HERMAN!?" they shouted. There was a look of disappointment in their eyes.

A few weeks later, I went back to the hatchery and I understood why. Because that's when I met Herman, the over-seventy-year-old, eleven-foot-long, five-hundred-pound white sturgeon.

He lives there in his own little man-made pond, surrounded by smaller sturgeon friends and children with their faces pressed against viewing windows. And to be honest, I was standing right alongside them.

Over the past twenty years, I've had a hard time dealing with the fact that I will never see a living dinosaur. Watching Herman pass back and forth across that pond was a pretty okay consolation prize.

After fifteen minutes of me gawking at Herman, the woman I brought was starting to get restless.* So, we got back in the car and headed to Hood River, Oregon, where we had a very nice day.

*Yes, I took a date to look at a big fish. Don't judge me.

On February 18th, 1971, the Portland Trail Blazers, then in their first season, were playing against the Los Angeles Lakers. The Lakers were ahead, it seemed all hope was lost. Then, guard Jim Barnett sank a shot from way downtown. Blazers announcer Bill Schonely, overcome with excitement, shouted: "Rip city! Alright!"

It had nothing to do with anything.

And it stuck.

Coffee

Portland and Seattle lead a pretty harmonious existence. They don't bicker. Their citizens visit each other regularly. They're happy being parts one and two of Pacific Northwest vacations.

But it seems that around the time of the Grunge movement, Seattle took a step forward. It became the "Big City," even though it's population isn't that much bigger than Portland's. And Portland was there screaming to the nation, "HEY! WE HAVE COOL BANDS, TOO!" But no one was listening.

Seattle took center stage and left Portland behind. That's when Portland said: "Okay, if that's the way it's going to be, we're going to fight back. We won't rest until we've taken the thing you hold most dear: coffee."

Cut to twenty years later: Portland has a shitload of coffee.

It seems like every few months, a new coffee place opens. And each is more intense than the last. The beans are somehow from a more pure source, the techniques have been handed down from generations in some remote land, the baristas are more serious about their craft than ever before. You'll hear this sentence a lot: "Oh that guy? He's a barista's barista."

And there's actually a coffee shop that's just called *Barista*, where it not only sells different kinds of coffee, it sells different brands of those different kinds. You won't order decaf if you know what's good for you.

And so it shall remain. The city will be ever filled with coffee shops until the day the world recognizes Portland as the equal of Seattle.

The better of Seattle would be nice, too.

Business Super Extra Casual

Q: What do you call someone wearing a suit in Portland?

A: Tourist.

Portland is the most casual major metropolitan area in America. Worries about being underdressed are almost non-existent here, especially for men. Thinking about wearing jeans to a wedding? You will not be the only one. Shorts? Sure, and why not make them cut-offs? A graphic tee is probably too much, but a plain one is just shy of formal. And don't even think about tucking it in.

How to explain this pervasive casualness? Perhaps it's because Portland is home to a surprising number of casual clothing companies. Nike, Columbia and Adidas are all headquartered here. As well as Keen. Is it possible to get more casual than Keen? No, it is not. Unless you're barefoot.

And since everyone knows someone who knows someone who works at one of these places and can get them into the half-price employee store, everyone wears that stuff all the time. Why buy an expensive suit jacket when a half-price Columbia fleece is almost the same thing if you squint hard enough from far enough away?

What about women, you may be asking. Do they dress up? They do. Which makes a night out to the symphony a fun game of wondering how all these immaculately dressed women can stand the fact that their husbands are wearing plaid shirts, unwashed denim, and technical sandals.

Cars

There was a two-month period where I forgot about my car. That's how good the buses are in this city and that's how easy it is to bike around. I owned a car and I just forgot about it for two months.

When I finally realized I still owned a car, it was like being in one of those dreams where you're in college. It's finals week and you've just remembered you have a class that you'd forgotten about all semester and the final is right now and if you don't get an A they're going to kick you out of school.

I hadn't laid eyes on my car. Was it parked around the corner? I had no idea. Would there be tickets? How much trouble was I in?

When I got home and found my car, I realized that I was wrong to worry. I was in Portland.

In what other city could you leave a car parked on the street for two months and still own a car? How was it not stolen? How was it not impounded? How did all of those windows remain unsmashed? How did roving bands of teenagers not even think to key it? How did I not get a single ticket?

I got in my car, started it up and moved it ten feet.

Then, I left it there for three weeks.

the '99 Subaru Legacy

A•K•A

"the Portland Escalade"

Crafting

Go ahead.

Make a joke about popsicle sticks.

Make fun of our glue and our glitter.

But just know that you risk finding a knitting needle jabbed into your eye.

Crafts are big here. For starters, hit the Portland Art Museum, which boasts an expansive collection of Native American art and crafts from the region. And then there's the craft scene with a capital *C*, an outgrowth of the city's strong D.I.Y. ethic that provides countless crafters a full-time job. They fill the shelves of stores all over town, from old favorites like the Pendleton Woolen Mill Store to members of the new craft guard such as Crafty Wonderland, which also hosts an epic hundreds-of-vendors sale at the convention center twice a year. And then there are craft beer, leather craft, and craft hot sauce scenes. (Which are things.)

A few years ago I needed a handyman, so I found one on Craigslist. He came, did his handyman thing, then casually mentioned he was also a hot-sauce maker. So I bought a bottle of his *Hot Winter Hot Sauce*. It was really good. Now you can buy it everywhere. And I get to brag and say I knew him back in the *making-it-in-his-kitchen* days.

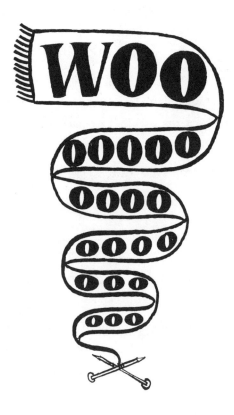

Good Old-Fashioned Fun

Though Portland has a somewhat dark, depraved history and quite a sophisticated present, you don't have to look hard to find the good old fashioned wholesome family fun.

Wanna go roller skating? Go to Oaks Park, one of the biggest and oldest roller skating rinks in the country. Sunday and Wednesday evenings are particularly festive, as older couples in matching velour skating outfits with their first names embroidered across their backs show up to skate to the music of the live organ.

Feel like some Skee-Ball? Electric Castle's Wunderland arcade is your spot. It'll cost you a couple bucks to get in, but once you are, all the games take nickels instead of quarters. That's right: nickels. They've got newfangled games as well as pinball, air hockey, Burger Time and that game where you try to drop a coin so that it knocks other coins off the ledge, but usually impossibly just stacks up on top of the other coins over and over and over again. This is also the place with the cheap movies, remember?

And if parades are your bag, be here in June and choose from the kid-friendly Grand Floral Rose Parade, the extra-kid-friendly Starlight party, and the Pride Parade a few weeks later, arguable the most kid friendly thanks to all the love and rainbows. And if you think Portlanders are too jaded to care about a parade, take your car out on the night before the Rose Parade and behold families camping out for a front row spot along the entire length of the parade route.

So go ahead and act like a kid. Having or being an actual kid welcome, but totally optional.

Food Carts

As I'm writing this, there are over-eight-hundred registered food carts in Multnomah County. Not all of them are in city limits. But believe me, a whole lot of them are. As soon as this book is released, that number will go up. Actually, that number will probably go up tomorrow, so let's just stick with "over-eight-hundred..." That sounds impressive enough, right?

More and more, when you walk down the street, you'll pass what was, until recently, an empty lot but now is filled with tiny trailers or little shacks, each serving a different kind of food. If Portland is one giant Shopping Mall, these are the food courts.

You'll find the most impressive collection downtown at SW 9th and Alder. A full city block of carts. All you have to do is walk around and take your pick. It sounds a lot easier than it is.

Cart indecision can be a real problem. If you are one of the lucky ones who can easily make a choice, look around you while you wait for your food. You'll see tourists bewildered by options. You'll see locals taking fake phone calls, walking up and down the block, trying to make it seem like they know what they're doing. You'll see the moment that a group of co-workers realizes that none of them want to go to the same place. Each one will end up walking back to the office alone. And you'll see old pros who've narrowed it down to their two favorite places. Their eyes dart back and forth as they weigh the pros and cons because at this moment, they're facing the most important decision in their lives.

People in other cities are used to seeing hot dog carts, fruit carts, maybe a Halal cart here and there. But in Portland, you get everything. One of my favorite pizzas in the city comes from a cart that's next to my favorite poutine, which is next to my favorite milkshake. It's a Cinnamon Toast Crunch milkshake. Jealous?

So why are there this many? The same reason restaurants are so jealous of them: You don't have to pay rent, you don't need to hire a staff, and to be successful, you only really have to know how to make one thing really well. Portland appreciates a specialty. The people don't just want to hear about where they should eat, they want to know what that place does better than anyone else.

Take Nong's on SW Alder. They make chicken on rice with a drinking broth. That's the menu. They can't offer you anything else. There's a line every day.

You hear about a place that makes a great thing, you go, you enjoy it on a bench and look at the cart across the way. Next time, you gotta try that place. The cycle continues.

Portland is not famous for its pizza.

It's good, if not really, really good. But there's no discernible style or mix of toppings we're known for.

But people in Portland treat pizza like it's the fifth food group. Sauce, cheese and crust are deconstructed and discussed in the reverent tone usually reserved for fine wine.

Portland artists make art about pizza. Portland bands write songs about pizza. And this was even before marijuana was legalized.

So grab a slice. Where? Anywhere. Because here's the thing that Portland understands like no other city: there's no such thing as bad pizza. Even an okay slice can take on any of those Michelin stars floating around the city.

Remember how people used to say that soccer was just never going to catch on in America?

Well they didn't count on one city:

Portland.

Portland loves soccer like Philadelphia loves steak and cheese.

The Timbers have an army that stands and sings the entire game. The Thorns draw a bigger crowd than any other women's sports team in the entire world.

The Timbers have Timber Joey, who cuts a round off a log with a chainsaw every time the Timbers score. The Thorns, not to be outdone, fire a cannon that shoots a cloud of thick pink smoke with every goal. Oh, and Portland State University boasts a women's team with multiple national titles and a lot of players who graduate to the U.S. National Team.

Unlike, say, American football fanatics, Portland practices what it preaches. Every park in Portland is filled with a youth soccer match virtually every weekend of the year. To work at a company of any size is to get the inevitable "We need an extra player for the 10pm game tonight" email.

To admit you don't like soccer, comment on how you wish there were more scoring in soccer, or refer to the "pitch" as the "field", or even innocently ask the difference between futsal and indoor soccer is to risk public shunning.

So ask the internet all your soccer related questions and keep your anti-soccer thoughts to yourself.

In the mid-to-late 1840s, Portland's population was growing fast. People were settling farther and farther away from the city and trees had to be cut down to make way for new roads. While there were plenty of workers to do the cutting, there was no one to remove the stumps. So, the stumps remained while the city waited for more manpower.

Some people walked on the stumps to avoid the mud. Some people painted the stumps white to make sure the city knew they were still there. When businessman John C. Ainsworth came to town in the early 1850s, he quipped that there were "more stumps than trees." No one was amused, but they figured it would be a good nickname.

Protests

As you've probably noticed, Portland has been in the news a lot lately for protesting.

You know what's so great about that statement? It doesn't matter if you read that twenty years ago, now, or twenty years from now, it pretty much always rings true.

We love to get fired up, hand paint some signs and get together with a few thousand of our closest friends and start chanting. There have been way too many great protests to mention, but here are two oldies but goodies.

During WWI, soldiers made ten cents a day while profiteers back home got rich. So Congress promised a bonus of one dollar for every day each soldier served to be delivered twenty years after the end of the war. Flash forward eight years to the middle of the depression and a lot of the former soldiers needed the money pronto. So a Portlander by the name of Walter Waters rallied his local V.A. to train-hop with him all the way to Washington D.C. to demand their bonuses. Their journey caught on and all told a "Bonus Army"* of seventeen-thousand veterans descended on D.C. and camped out for weeks. Instead of the bonuses, they got the National Guard rousting them out of the city. But Congress did pass the G.I. Bill.

Cut to the mid-90s and a bunch of Reed students heard that Vice President Dan Quayle was slated to speak at a fancy fundraising event downtown. So they dyed some mashed potatoes red and some blue, while others not at all. Then they each ate as much as they possibly could and headed downtown. The plan was to storm the gates and gloriously vomit red white and blue in an effort to ruin the event. Unfortunately, they were denied access as it was a $1000-a-plate dinner, so they did their throwing up outside. The potatoes didn't quite resurface in the full spectrum of patriotic colors as anticipated, but central planner Igor Vamos did go on to form the Yes Men.

*For the full story, read *The Bonus Army: an American Epic* by Andrew's Dad, Paul Dickson and Thomas B. Allen.

Japanese Garden

If you find yourself walking around the Japanese Garden thinking: "Wow, this feels pretty authentic," good thinking. It's widely regarded as the most authentic Japanese Garden outside of Japan.

The Garden was created as an olive branch after WWII as Portland and Japan started doing business together. Landscape architect Takuma Tono was hired and rather than create a single style of garden, he created five, representing different time periods and gardening approaches.

It is without question one of the most serene places in the city and there's never been a better time to visit as the Garden has gone through a massive expansion.

So get on up there, relax, be at peace and walk off whatever happened at the dive bar the night before.

QUIETLY

Judging

You know how on the East Coast, if you're discussing politics and everyone agrees, someone will take the opposing view just for the sake of having a spirited debate?

Yeah, that just doesn't happen here.

We are not especially confrontational here in Portland.

When met with someone who has an opinion we disagree with, instead of getting into an argument, we're far more likely to stay mum until the person leaves and then explode with indignation and vehemently make our dissenting points once we're sure everyone within earshot agrees with us.

So, if you say something vaguely controversial and see someone cross their arms, furrow their brow, and mumble "hmm..." in reaction—or even worse, say nothing but look kind of constipated—go ahead and give them a hug and say you're sorry, even if you're not.

See how easy this masking your true feelings thing is!

Alternative Beverages

Sure, Portland has your run-of-the-mill beverages just like any other city, but for us, it's just not enough. We really enjoy getting weird with the liquids we toss down our collective gullet.

Kombucha? We drink more than water itself.

Drinking vinegars? Of course! Would you prefer Tamarind, Turmeric or Blood Orange?

Kava? There's a great spot serving nothing but over on Division.

Ginger Beer? The place that only sells that is ten blocks over on Hawthorne.

Hard Cider? Or as we call it: Cider? There are bars all across the city that serve nothing but.

We can't even do normal drinks normally. Walk into the beer aisle of the seediest-looking corner store and you'll have to walk past vastly different genre's of IPAs, beer brewed with peach, pumpkin, and vanilla beans, and a cooler of Belgian style ales before you'll see a six pack of Bud.

If you're lookin' for a normal drink at a normal bar, we suggest you start gettin' weird as soon as possible.

what DO you DO?

That dreaded question.

The sign that the conversation in which you find yourself has long since reached its zenith.

From now on, you are no longer connecting as human beings, but as titles and bank accounts.

Except, that is, when you're in Portland.

In most places when someone asks you what you do, they're really trying to figure out how important it is for them to keep talking to you. If your career can help their career.

But when someone asks you in Portland, they don't want to know what your job is. They're asking what you like to do. And they are completely and genuinely interested because if they like doing what you like doing, there is a very good chance they will want to do it with you. Both literally and possibly also literally in a different, sexier way.

> **You**: "What do you do?"

> **Me**: "I like exploring different hiking trails in the Columbia River Gorge."

> **You**: "Great, let's go this weekend."

> **Me**: "Cool. I also enjoy canning the vegetables I grow in my backyard."

> **You**: "I have more tomatoes than I can handle, can you give me some tips?"

> **Me**: "Absolutely. And in the bedroom, I'm into sci-fi role play."

> **You**: "My house is two blocks away."

> **Me**: "Let's go."

Why stay in and look at a screen when you have this awesome city full of amazing people to do things you'd like to do with?

the Swifts

Vaux's Swift is a very small bird that likes to nest in chimneys all over the West Coast.

In the last week of September, thousands of them set up camp in the chimney of Chapman Elementary School in NW Portland.

Every night of that week, they return to the chimney after a day of hunting insects. But they don't return one at a time. They show up in a giant, swirling swarm. They circle the school, then form a funnel and disappear inside.

It's stunning.

This is an attraction. People pack picnic dinners and arrive early with their lawn chairs and blankets. They're not only there to see the swifts. They're there to celebrate the last event of summer. When this week is over, those lawn chairs won't see the light of day for a long, long time.

It's a perfect way to end on a high note. To sit back with some potato salad and reflect on all those trips to the river, all those barbecues, all those cornhole tournaments. It's a goodbye to summer.

And then, there are the hawks.

When the swifts are circling the chimney, local hawks take notice. They like eating swifts and every night, they'll catch a few. The audience's reaction to this natural act says a lot about Portland:

They boo.

When you're in Portland, you never really have to deal with anything you hate. It's pleasant. It's bike paths and bakeries and community art centers and all the cheap beer you can handle. People love it here because they don't have to feel bad. So when they see a nice bird die, they say: "BOOOO, I came to watch that nice bird do a nice thing!"

This is what makes Portland a magical place to live. It's what makes you a softer, more sensitive person. Whether that's a good or bad thing, I'll leave up to you.

Oh, there are always a few people who cheer on the hawk. Portland is also about being a rebel.

References

Pine State Biscuits

They make biscuits. They're really good. Pine State has a number of brick & mortar locations that I'm sure are easily discoverable to you. The important thing here is that they all have the same hours (except Farmers Market):

Monday to Sunday 7am to 3pm

Laurelhurst Theater

It's just a great second run theater. They even show one classic a week. I saw *Groundhog Day* there. Just go.

2735 East Burnside Street Portland, OR 97214

Avalon Theatre & Wunderland

The Avalon is in an arcade called Electric Castle's Wunderland. From the outside, it looks like a clown porn theater.

3451 SE Belmont Street Portland, OR 97214-4246
Sunday to Friday 12pm to 12am
Saturdays 11am to 12am

Sassy's Bar & Grill

Sassy's is the default strip club for everyone I know. It has a really high, unfinished ceiling, which makes it feel like you're in a sexy, sexy barn.

927 SE Morrison Street Portland, OR 97214
Everyday 10:30am to 2:30am

Lovely's Fifty Fifty

Wood-fired pizza and housemade ice cream. If they didn't close, would you ever leave? It was here that I had my first taste of salted caramel and my taste buds have been thanking me ever since.

4039 N Mississippi Avenue Portland, OR 97217
Tuesday to Sunday 5pm to 10pm

Powell's City of Books

Powell's has a number of locations, but there's only one true City of Books. Have fun getting lost in it.

1005 Burnside Street Portland, OR 97209
Everyday 9am to 11pm

Salt & Straw

Their empire is quickly spreading across the Western seaboard, but I remember visiting the original location on NW 23rd and having my mind blown by balsamic ice cream.

838 NW 23rd Avenue Portland, OR 97210
Everyday 10am to 11pm

Crafty Wonderland

If you are crafty, thought about being crafty, or have ever appreciated a craft of any kind, this shop is for you. They also hold markets around the city from time to time.

808 SW 10th Avenue Portland, OR 97205
Everyday 10am to 6pm

Portland Japanese Garden

Relax.

611 SW Kingston Avenue Portland, OR 97205
Tuesday to Sunday 10am to 7pm
Monday 12pm to 7pm

Pendleton

Pendleton isn't so much a place as a state of mind. But it actually is a city in Eastern Oregon and the woolen mills named after that actual place have a number of locations and stockists across North America. I have two of their blankets on my bed at this exact moment. One of which I used as reference to create that weird pizza illustration.

www.pendleton-usa.com

Cartopia

This is where you'll find Pyro Pizza (an amazing pizza), Potato Champion (amazing poutine), and a number of other amazing, movable eateries.

1204 SE Hawthorne Blvd Portland, OR 97214
Tuesday to Sunday 12pm to 12am

Oaks Amusement Park

If you need a roller rink that's been around for over a century, look no further.

7805 SE Oaks Park Way Portland, OR 97202

oakspark.com

The Bonneville Hatchery

Apparently, the best time to visit is October through
November. You'll see a bunch of salmon spawning then.
I say go whenever.

70543 NE Herman Loop Cascade Locks, OR 97014

Hood River, Oregon

It's just a nice town. There's a great Brewery there called Double Mountain. Take a significant
other and make a day of it.

Keep Portland Weird

Even though Portland is pretty normal, you can get your very own bumper sticker at:

www.keepportlandweird.com

The Swifts

It's amazing. Bring a camera.

Chapman Elementary School
1445 NW 26th Ave Portland, OR 97210